Prayers and Praise in Poetic Phrase: Volume Four

Prayers for our Children

R. J. Shy

DEDICATION

I dedicate this book to my dear grandmother, Maggie Blair Davis Shy, who lived to be ninety-eight years old. Although she departed her body May 24, 2020, to be present with the Lord, her legacy lives on through her children, grandchildren, great grand children, and great, great grandchildren.

CONTENTS

CONTENTS

.

ACKNOWLEDGMENTS

I'd like to acknowledge my lovely wife, Chalindia Shy, whose patience and understanding has allowed me to complete this volume.

My son, ***forget*** not my law; but let thine heart keep my
commandments:
(Proverbs 3:1)

*F*orgive my procrastination,
*O*rdered steps, I've failed to take.
*R*egardless of the situation,
*G*race my heart, to not forsake.
*E*ducating my children, is my responsibility.
*T*each me to be faithful, in Jesus's name, as I honor Thee.

*F*ather, I thank You, for all You do.
*O*bstacles attempt, to distract from You.
*R*emind my children, to put You first.
*G*ive them hunger and thirst, for chapter and verse.
*E*ven though this world, has an ungodly aim,
*T*each my children to follow You, in Jesus's name.

My son, forget not my law; but let ***thine heart keep*** my
commandments:
(Proverbs 3:1)

*T*he only way to You, is through Christ, Your only begotten Son.
*H*elp them to realize, that there is no other one.
*I*ncrease their desire, to seek Your holy face,
*N*ot living for the moment, but living by Your grace.
*E*quip them, in Jesus's name, that they may, endure the race.

*H*eavenly Father, I give You my children,
*E*ach and every part.
*A*nd ask You to, lead their precious, little hearts.
*R*escue from temptations; lest they be pulled in.
*T*each them, in Jesus's name, to imitate Christ, as dear children.

*K*ingdom business first, for in You we stand.
*E*very word and deed, should honor Your commands.
*E*ven when they are tempted, to stray from Your hands.
*P*lace within my children, pure desires, in Jesus's name, amen.

My son, forget not my law; but let thine heart keep my
commandments:
(Proverbs 3:1)

Circumstances challenge, temptations are within, and around us,
Offering alternative plans, that their wiles may confound us.
Making attempts to distract, they introduce ungodly plans.
Make my children resistant, as they keep Your commands.
Anoint their eyes, that they may see, according to Your word.
Navigating about their enemies, grace godly discernment to be stirred.
Direct their steps, as they listen, clearly.
Many exhibit a form of godliness, but fail to walk sincerely.
Entertaining sin, for they fear no recompense;
Nevertheless, I pray my children walk, according to Your word, without pretense.
Teach them to submit, and walk within Your Spirit.
Sanctify, in Jesus's name, as they hear Your voice, and fear it.

For **length** of **days**, and **long** life, and peace, shall they add to thee.
(Proverbs 3:2)

Lord, teach my children to honor You,
Even through trials, and life long pursuits.
Never hating Your rebuke,
Grace them to love correction too.
Teach my children, as I lead by example.
Heal and reveal Your will, as You are tasted, tested, and sampled.

Danger is sneaky, like a rat for cheese.
And brings the fearful, to their knees.
Yet, those who trust, within the Son.
Sing songs of safety, for Christ has won!

Lord, bless me to model, Your righteousness,
Observing Your word, that my home may be blessed.
Nevertheless, my children, must give an account.
Grant me grace to disciple; lest Your word, they discount.

For length of days, and long *life*, and *peace*, *shall* they add to thee.
(Proverbs 3:2)

Living within Christ, brings persecution.
Isolation can deceive: disrupt clear resolution.
Fill my children, with faith to endure:
Effectual, fervent prayers, in Jesus's name, in obedience, keeps them pure.

Place an unwavering, godly fear within them.
Even as their desires and Your word, become synonym.
Allow them to stand, as they love You much more.
Challenge their faith, as a loving mentor.
Equip, my children, in Jesus's name, for spiritual war.

Solely, my help, as I cling to Christ.
Heavenly Father, heal my wounds, for I have been sliced.
As You work, through me, without restraint,
Let my children observe; lest they grow weary and faint.
Let me be an example, in Jesus's name, without complaint.

For length of days, and long life, and peace, shall *they* add to *thee*.
(Proverbs 3:2)

Teach my children, to love You, with their whole heart.
Humbly and honestly, as they yield every part.
Even as temptation challenges them,
You can grace them to overcome every emotional whim.

Teach my children, to love You, with their whole heart.
Humbly and honestly, as they yield every part.
Even as this world attempts, to make them conform,
Equip them to be transform, in Jesus's name, against worldly norm.

Prayers and Praise in Poetic Phrase: Volume Four

Let not ***mercy*** and truth forsake thee: bind them about thy neck;
write them upon the table of thine heart:
(Proverbs 3:3)

*M*ake a heart of flesh reside, within their stony parts.
*E*veryone falls short, sin has stained every chart.
*R*emind them of forgiveness, grace, and Christ's requirement.
*C*hange their paradigm, regardless of their current environment.
*Y*ou are our role model, in Jesus's name, impart grace, for fleshly
retirement.

Let not mercy and ***truth*** forsake thee: bind them about thy neck;
write them upon the table of thine heart:
(Proverbs 3:3)

*T*here are many voices heard,
*R*ighteous, in their own eyes,
*U*ndermining the living word,
*T*eaching falsely, they spread their lies.
*H*elp my children to heed Christ, in Jesus's name, with no compromise.

Let not mercy and truth ***forsake thee***: bind them about thy neck;
write them upon the table of thine heart:
(Proverbs 3:3)

Father, help me model true Christianity.
Overflow from my belly, funnel to their hearts through me.
Renew within me a clean heart.
Sanctify and consecrate every moving part.
As I teach them of their responsibility:
Knocking, seeking, asking, and abiding within Thee;
Empower them, in Jesus's name, to walk within spiritual liberty.

Teach them to follow Christ, for He is the only way.
Help them to self deny; lest their flesh leads them astray.
Even as they are tempted, to maneuver left or right,
Enable my children, in Jesus's name, with the power of Your might.

Let not mercy and truth forsake thee: ***bind*** them about thy neck;
write them upon the table of thine heart:
(Proverbs 3:3)

Bless my children to forgive, all who've caused offense.
In Jesus's name I ask, be their esteem and confidence.
None is too great a task, for You are Lord of all.
Dress their hearts, with grace, to humbly answer Your call.

Let not mercy and truth forsake thee: bind ***them*** about thy neck;
write them upon the table of thine heart:
(Proverbs 3:3)

To forgive the unforgivable is impossible to do.
Heal their broken hearts, as they love and honor You.
Endow my children with Your love, as they look toward the hills.
Meditation on Your word, as they obey, will keep them healed.

Let not mercy and truth forsake thee: bind them **about** thy neck;
write them upon the table of thine heart:
(Proverbs 3:3)

As we meditate on Matthew, twenty five, we see a need for
preparation.
Because all will stand before Jesus, to receive eternal citation.
Oil is necessary, for substance is required.
Unrepented hearts, will be directed to the fire.
Teach my children,in Jesus's name, that sin, within Christ, must be
retired.

Let not mercy and truth forsake thee: bind them about thy **neck**;
write them upon the table of thine heart:
(Proverbs 3:3)

No one, outside of Christ, can follow right, bless my children, with
supernatural affection.
Emitting a darkness, which drowns light: unhealthy introspection,
Causes my children to surrender in flight, like a prey of rejection.
Keep them full of Your radiance: bright, Spirit filled direction.

Let not mercy and truth forsake thee: bind them about thy neck;
write them upon the table of thine heart:
(Proverbs 3:3)

Water erodes a rock in time:
Repetitive contact.
I ask You to renew them, with a made up mind.
Teach my children, to abide within Christ, the true vine.
Even as they've fallen short, and have misused multiple life lines.

Let not mercy and truth forsake thee: bind them about thy neck;
write ***them upon*** the ***table*** of thine heart:
(Proverbs 3:3)

*T*he words You speak, are all we need.
*H*elp my children, as Your rivers, flow through me.
*E*ncourage their hearts, as we share each day,
*M*aking it a practice for us, to meditate and pray.

*U*se my children, for Your glory, however You see fit.
*P*lace within them peace, as they humbly submit.
*O*perating by emotion, is total vanity.
*N*evertheless, in Jesus's name, bless them to maneuver, by Your Spirit,
fluently.

*T*each them Your word, that they may grow.
*A*nd bless my children, to submit, to what they know.
*B*ecause of sin and iniquity,
*L*ove has grown cold, considerably.
*E*ven as You are Almighty, bless them to live it out, by Your ability, grace
them to conquer doubt, in Jesus's name, deliberately.

Let not mercy and truth forsake thee: bind them about thy neck;
write them upon the table of ***thine*** heart:
(Proverbs 3:3)

*T*hough they have responsibility, godly desire comes from You.
*H*elp them to be faithful, to what You've called them to.
*I*ncrease Your holy presence, as they humbly obey.
*N*evertheless, convict; lest they forget along the way.
*E*ven as they maneuver, avoiding the compromise of the day.

Prayers and Praise in Poetic Phrase: Volume Four

Let not mercy and truth forsake thee: bind them about thy neck;
write them upon the table of thine *heart*:
(Proverbs 3:3)

*H*earing deceptive voices, which attack from every side,
*E*ach day the battle rages, for they also struggle with their pride.
*A*ll play a part, for none can hide, for temptations present themselves,
from within and outside.
*R*eviewing your holy pages, bless them to consider sin's wages.
*T*each my children to honor You, in Jesus's name, through their various,
sensitive stages.

So *shall thou* find favor and good understanding in the sight of God and
man.
(Proverbs 3:4)

*S*how my Children the benefit of,
*H*umbly walking in agape love.
*A*s the lies of the past, attempt to maim,
*L*ead them to victory, in Jesus's name.
*L*et them serve You with joy, and without shame.

*T*each my children of, their responsibility to be,
*H*umbly acceptable unto Thee,
*O*ut of the power of the Spirit.
*U*nderstanding will come, as they are willing to hear it.

So shall thou *find* favor and good understanding in the sight of God and
man
(Proverbs 3:4)

*F*ather, I thank You for my children, sometimes a blessing in disguise.
I ask that You grace me to model, true Christ like living, without
compromise.
*N*evertheless, for Your glory, even as I struggle to give You praise,
*D*irect, as I stay focused, in Jesus's name, within Your ways.

So shall thou find ***favor*** and ***good*** understanding in the sight of God and man
(Proverbs 3:4)

Fearing You, Heavenly Father, leads to faith, which leads to favor.
Adhering to faithful creeds, only seeds toward good behavior.
Voices bombard my children, to steer them from our Savior,
Ordering, demanding that they sample many worldly flavors.
Redirect them to Christ, in Jesus's name, and to ever love their neighbor.

Grace my children to have a heavenly view.
Others push and pull, that they may see things as they do.
Open their eyes, by Your Holy Spirit.
Direct them, in Jesus's name, as they are willing to hear it.

So shall thou find favor and good **understanding** in the sight of God and
man
(Proverbs 3:4)

Under every circumstance, the flesh desires a thrill.
Nevertheless, as it knows best, to lust against Your holy will.
During frustrations, of various kinds,
Evil will express, if it resides within the mind.
Remind my children that the battle starts, long before the test.
Strategies, of the Spirit, provide preemptive peace and rest.
The mist of the battle, is not the proper time.
And the lack of meditation, does not change one's paradigm.
Now is the time, to seek with their whole heart.
Direct their Intellect, as they surrender every part.
I ask that You would grace me, to exhibit Christlike, godliness.
Neutrality is not an option, for You require more than this.
Grace me, in Jesus's name, to exemplify redemptive evidence.

So shall thou find favor and good understanding in the **sight** of God and
man
(Proverbs 3:4)

Societal pressures can overwhelm.
It's impossible to keep sin at bay, utilizing a fleshly dam.
Grace my children to know You as "I Am",
Heal their hearts, for at times, I sank, following my own program.
Touch every part, for You can reach even secret realms.

Trust in the *Lord with* all thine heart; and lean not unto thine own
understanding.
(Proverbs 3:5)

*T*here is no other help, Heavenly Father.
*R*esting on anything else is a bother.
*U*seless are tools, and strategies falter.
*S*tamina fails to fulfill or alter.
*T*each my children, in Jesus's name, to build themselves a daily altar.

*L*eading my children to develop worldly coping skills,
*O*nly perpetuates and reinforces what they perceived to be real.
*R*enew, within Your truth, as they seek You wholeheartedly.
*D*irect, in Jesus's name, as they surrender every part to Thee.

*W*orshipers worship in Spirit and truth,
*I*n step with Christ, as they bare good fruit.
*T*each my children the value of
*H*umbly repenting, as they live by Your love.

Trust in the Lord with all *thine* heart; and lean not unto thine own
understanding.
(Proverbs 3:5)

*T*each me to present my body, as a living sacrifice.
*H*oliness is required, as I abide within Christ.
I desire to be a living epistle, for my child to read.
*N*evertheless, I pray You bless, me to seek You, as a need
*E*quip me, in Jesus's name, to walk within humility.

Prayers and Praise in Poetic Phrase: Volume Four

Trust in the Lord with all thine **heart**; and **lean** not **unto** thine own
understanding.
(Proverbs 3:5)

Heavenly Father, my heart, has not been right at times,
Even as I've acted out, of ungodly paradigms.
As a result, my children have suffered, to some degree.
Restore what I have wasted, when I've focused less on Thee.
Teach me to put You first, and all else secondly.

Leaning on a crutch, does not deliver.
Even though, it may temporarily soothe; it undermines the giver.
Abiding within You, is where their power lies.
Navigate my children beyond weariness, in Jesus's name, and the waves
of compromise.

Until Christ reigns, there is no peace.
Nevertheless, my children must decrease.
Talking and walking, within Christ, is where there is gain.
Open their hearts, by Your grace, in Jesus's name.

Trust in the Lord with all thine heart; and lean not unto **thine** own
understanding.
(Proverbs 3:5)

They may not understand Your paradigm.
Hearing, according to Your word, takes patience and time
Increase their capacity to deny self.
Nevertheless, for their best works, without Christ, lead to death.
Enable my children, in Jesus's name, to choose spiritual height and
depth.

Trust in the Lord with all thine heart; and lean not unto thine own
understanding.
(Proverbs 3:5)

*U*nder pressure from every side,
*N*arrow leads to life, but destruction is wide.
*D*irect my children, though voices are demanding.
*E*stablish my children, with godly understanding.
*R*emind me of my responsibility.
*S*end revival, in Jesus's name, let it began with me.
*T*each me how to avoid, provoking my children to wrath,
*A*nd how to nurture and love, on Your behalf.
*N*ow You are needed, more than ever before.
*D*raw us closer to You, more and more.
*I*n all things , let us give thanks.
*N*avigate us through evil, and descending ranks.
*G*rant them, in Jesus's name, to live as, new born, saints.

In all thy ***ways*** acknowledge him, and he shall direct thy paths.
(Proverbs 3:6)

*W*hatever pleases You is best.
*A*lign their goals, with Your righteousness.
*Y*et, my children must choose the same.
*S*atisfy, as they seek, to live within Jesus's precious name.

Prayers for our Children

In all thy ways ***acknowledge*** him, and he ***shall*** direct thy paths.
(Proverbs 3:6)

Almighty God, Your love is real,
Caused not by what I think or feel.
Keep my heart in league with You.
Navigate all I say and do.
Observing all the world's demands,
Will keep me bound, within the land.
Lead my children with Christ's commands.
Ever keep them, within Your loving hands.
Declaring Your word is key.
Grace them to live obediently.
Empower, in Jesus's name, them and me.

Show my children their identity:
Heavenly citizens, for Christ has redeemed.
Although this world attempts to taint their view,
Let them see themselves within You.
Loving righteousness, as You are their pursuit.

In all thy ways acknowledge him, and he shall ***direct*** thy ***paths***.
(Proverbs 3:6)

Deception is a beast, which seems to mean no harm.
It maneuvers slowly, closer, with it's luster and charm.
Retrain my children, to recognize alarms,
Even when the enemy, attempts to disarm.
Condition my children, in Jesus's name,
To remain ever faithful to Your word, without shame.

Please bless my children to avoid,
Alternative paths I should have destroyed.
Temptations I should have conquered well,
Have hindered, and pulled them to rebel.
Strengthen them, in Jesus's name, that their testimony, may not be the same.

Be not *wise* in *thine* own eyes: fear the Lord, and depart from evil.
(Proverbs 3:7)

*W*hen Your word is no, bless them to accept it.
*I*f a feeling contradicts You, grace them to reject it.
*S*ettle their hearts, within Your ways,
*E*ven as challenges come, via phrase or phase.

*T*his world has a wisdom, which dishonors You.
*H*ell enlarges itself to receive.
I pray that my children, stay within Your truth.
*N*avigate; lest they fail to believe.
*E*ven grace them, in Jesus's name, to be a light, to the innocent, and naive.

Prayers and Praise in Poetic Phrase: Volume Four

Be not wise in thine own *eyes*: fear the Lord, and depart from evil.
(Proverbs 3:7)

*E*ve allowed her eyes to deceive,
*Y*ielding to what she thought would relieve.
*E*ven as my children seek less stress,
*S*trengthen their faith, and reveal, Your true happiness.

Be not wise in thine own eyes: *fear* the *Lord*, and *depart* from evil.
(Proverbs 3:7)

*F*alse evidence appearing real,
*E*ducates my children, that they can't be healed.
*A*llow them to see, the reality:
*R*especting the Son, makes restoration an actuality.

*L*usts of the flesh will mislead: fight to rule.
*O*utside wiles will attempt to school.
*R*emind my children of Your power to,
*D*estroy the soul and body too.

*D*isciples of Christ live a life of repentance,
*E*lected, for Christ, through His blood, accomplished remittance.
*P*racticing the deeds, which put Christ on the cross,
*A*ssures that a soul is definitely lost.
*R*emind my children of His sacrificial love,
*T*hat they may submit, to the power thereof.

Be not wise in thine own eyes: fear the Lord, and depart *from evil*.
(Proverbs 3:7)

*F*orce is not used to solicit a soul.
*R*epentance is not the result, of God taking total control.
*O*ne must decide to humble themselves.
*M*ortifying ones members, in Christ, is to put away self.

*E*yes looking left to right, decide according to their sight,
(*V*alidating their own truth, as I compare themselves to you).
I pray that You bless my children to,
*L*ove justice, according to Your view.

It **shall** be health to thy navel, and marrow to thy bones.
(Proverbs 3:8)

Satisfaction is only found within You.
Help me to model love, according to Your truth.
As I let my light shine before them,
Love can infiltrate, as Your word and my heart, become synonym.
Lord, in Jesus's name, grace me to love like Christ, without fleshly bias,
or emotional whim.

Prayers for our Children

It shall be **health** to thy **navel**, and marrow to thy bones.
(Proverbs 3:8)

Having a form of godliness, but denying the power thereof,
Enables the flesh to rule, contrary to His Spirit of love.
As my children repent, as Christ has called them to,
Love will rule their hearts, as their mind is renewed.
Teach my children, to walk within Your light.
Help them, in Jesus's name, to be strong, within Your might.

No one understands like You,
And everything they go through.
Victorious are we, as we obey,
Even as life fails to go our way.
Lord, bless my children, in Jesus's name, to follow Your word, without
shame.

It shall be health to thy navel, and **marrow** to thy **bones**.
(Proverbs 3:8)

My heart can be deceptive
And deceive even me.
Renew my main directive.
Refresh with liberty.
Organize my home, let my children see.
Walking in the Spirit, can be reality.

Bless my children to understand,
Overcomers live within Your commands.
Never are Your boundaries present, solely to restrain.
Equip us, by Your Spirit, be our wealth and gain.
Satisfy them, as they trust You, in Jesus's holy name.

Honor the **Lord with** thy substance, and with the firstfruits of all thine
increase:
(Proverbs 3:9)

Help my children to be faithful, for they temporarily.
Officiate, administrate, talents arbitrarily.
Now is preparation, for eternity.
Overcoming temporal treasures, produces spiritual maturity.
Renew their mind, in Jesus's name, resulting in godly purity.

Luke chapter nine, verse sixty two,
Omits ones name, from the book of life, for judgment will ensue.
Revive my children, as they seek You, with their whole heart.
Disciple, in Jesus's name, as they surrender every part.

When my children remember, that You are boss,
Increase can manifest, as they carry their cross.
Teach them to be faithful, with everything You've given.
Heal, in Jesus's name; lest they mistake gain, for godly living.

Prayers and Praise in Poetic Phrase: Volume Four

Honor the Lord with thy **substance**, and with the firstfruits of all thine
increase:
(Proverbs 3:9)

Storing treasure on earth, where moth can corrupt,
Undermines self sacrifice, leading to loss and disgust.
Bless my children to maintain, an eternal perspective.
Satisfy, as they maneuver, according to Your directives.
Teach them to seek, to please Your heart,
As they deny self interests, to surrender every part.
Navigate, as they contemplate, the carrying of their cross.
Convict, as they consider, our Saviour's cost.
Envelop and secure, in Jesus's name; lest their soul is tossed.

Honor the Lord with thy substance, and **with** the firstfruits of all thine
increase:
(Proverbs 3:9)

Wisdom reveals, that money is a tool.
If it were a god, it would act without heart, and be cruel.
Teach my children, of it's proper use.
Heal their hearts; lest inward parts, condone material abuse.

Honor the Lord with thy substance, and with the ***firstfruits*** of all thine
increase:
(Proverbs 3:9)

Faithful are those, who honor You first,
In step with meditation, upon Chapter and verse.
Reverence is due, in every arena.
Starting now, bless my children to bow, for their motives, will be
subpoenaed.
Trusting You, in Jesus's name, with a thankful demeanor.
Forgetting that You, give the increase,
Reinforces a lack of reverence, and perpetual decrease.
Understanding is key, in all we do.
I pray that You bless, my children to,
Trust that You will reward, financial faithfulness.
Submission, in Jesus's name, that their accounts, may be blessed.

Honor the Lord with thy substance, and with the firstfruits of all ***thine***
increase:
(Proverbs 3:9)

Teach my children, to honor You first.
Humbly, financially; lest their purse is cursed.
Inconsistency or consistency, in faithful giving, is not salvational.
Nevertheless, obedience, in this area, is a necessity and graduational.
Emancipate them, in Jesus's name, from erroneous paradigms, which
are merely generational.

Honor the Lord with thy substance, and with the firstfruits of all thine
increase:
(Proverbs 3:9)

Increase manifests, according to Your will.
Now may not be the time, for certain things to fulfill.
Can they continue, when patience is required?
Reverting to the flesh, does not accomplish Your desires.
Evil is prepared to direct at any time.
As we cast down ungodly imaginations, we adjust our paradigm.
Satisfy my children, as they navigate Your ways.
Even when You tarry, or they experience delays.

So **shall** thy barns be filled with plenty, and thy presses shall burst out with new wine.

(Proverbs 3:10)

Secure the connection, between You and them.
Heal wounds from the past, that Your word, and their heart, become synonym.
As You bless them, compromise is not exempt.
Let them see Your value; lest they view You with contempt.
Lead, by Your Spirit, for the enemy preempts.

So shall thy **barns** be filled with plenty, and thy presses shall burst out with new wine.

(Proverbs 3:10)

Bless them to do business, according to Your will.
As they cast down wicked notions, grace them to cling, to what is real.
Receiving what they sow, for You are not mocked,
Nevertheless, let them obey; lest their blessings are blocked.
Satisfy, for Your glory, in Jesus's name, as they continually knock.

So shall thy barns be **filled** with **plenty**, and thy **presses** shall burst out with new wine.

(Proverbs 3:10)

Foundations which are built on You,
Increase in glory, find strength, and renew.
Lack is not the portion, of Your children.
Let love motivate, my children, as they give in.
Every empty space, within their heart,
Decreases as they submit, wholeheartedly; not in part.

Place within them, the value of truth.
Let Your love penetrate, as your words renew.
Even as their substance increases, for Your glory.
Navigate, as they live, in obedience to Your story.
Teach them to be faithful, and endure to the end.
You can satisfy my children, in Jesus's name, as they repent of their sin.

Persecution is a part of righteous living.
Rightly Responding to Your love, results in generous giving.
Even as Your Spirit contradicts,
Senses which hate the crucifix,
Settle my children, as they repent.
Equip them with godly confidence.
Sowing and reaping is a principle, that You have fixed.

So shall thy barns be filled with plenty, and thy presses **shall burst** out **with** new **wine**.

(Proverbs 3:10)

Seasons of increase can overwhelm.
Healthy wallets and purses, can suffocate the damned.
As my children seek to honor You.
Let their motives be honest and true;
Lest wealth manifests rotten fruit.

Believing that work, is no necessity,
Unprepared sluggards, take advantage of generosity.
Relying on manipulation, they stay afloat.
Securing nothing, still their egos bloat.
Teach my children, that the faithful, are who You promote.

Wealth is a tool, to be used, for Your glory,
If it is placed, within the correct, category.
The proper rule over it, can establish Your covenant.
Heal my children, by Your word, as they confess and repent.

When You are our agenda, we are complete.
In the mist of adversity, and various degrees, of heat
Nothing can separate, from Your love.
Ensure my children, that You are enough.

My son, *despise* not the *chastening* of the **Lord**; neither be weary of His
correction:
(Proverbs 3:11)

Discipline corrects, for You are love.
Even though the sorrow flows, we know the truth thereof.
So, bastards have no father, but we are legitimate sons.
Practicing Your law, within our hearts, as the elect, chosen ones.
I ask that You'd heal the wounds, as they confess the pain inside.
Still, emotions will lie, as self love, promotes pride.
Empower my children, in Jesus's name, to trust Your word, as their
guide.

Choosing to obey Your word is best,
Hating the filth of wickedness.
As Your Spirit convicts, grace them to hear,
So that the rod, can be spared, as they walk within godly fear.
Touching a body, that the soul may be saved,
Edifies within love, as they misbehave.
Nevertheless, bless them to fear,
In and out of season, making their election clear.
Grace them to respect Your boundaries, for the consequences of
rejecting Christ, are extremely severe.

Learning from the witnesses, which served You before,
Observing that You disciplined, that they may bare fruit and more.
Reveal to my children, that love does restrict.
Direct their day, in every way, as their hearts can handle it.

My son, despise not the chastening of the Lord; *neither* be *weary* of His
correction:
(Proverbs 3:11)

*N*ow, as the Holy Spirit whispers,
*E*ven before the gentleness, intensifies, becoming crisper,
*I*ncrease within them wisdom, to confess their concern,
*T*o get it right, repent, delight, for Your word alone is stern.
*H*elp them humble themselves; lest they are bruised,
*E*ven if momentarily, it appears, as if they lose.
*R*ejecting the optics, let Your fear be what they choose.

*W*hen a childish individual, does not get their way,
*E*motional responses, will show their heart's decay.
*A*s my children mature, to discern Your will,
*R*ighteousness will rule, much more than what they feel.
*Y*ou are the answer, in Jesus's name, restore my children and heal.

*C*oncerning correction, though it's difficult to see,
*O*bserving our need, You respond compassionately.
*R*emind them to love Your word, for it heals,
*R*estores, strengthens, and reveals.
*E*ven when they error, Your word is law.
*C*hrist became a curse, though He lived without flaw.
*T*each my children to love Your correction.
*I*t's a necessity, for their own protection.
*O*pen wide their hearts; lest they ignore.
*N*avigation towards redemption and much, much more.

For **whom** the **Lord loveth** he correcteth; even as a father the son in
whom he delighteth.
(Proverbs 3:12)

Wiles will come to pass, from every direction.
Help my children be humble, for their own protection.
Obedience and repentance, are paramount,
Made righteous, for Christ paid our sin account.

Loving correction, is a wise decision.
Observing Your ways, sharpens spiritual percision.
Revive my children, as they follow Christ.
Direct, in Jesus's name, for rebellion is overpriced.

Lust will destroy, without restraint.
Orders from the flesh, manipulate the saint.
Vanities will distract.
Emotions will lead them, to over react.
Teach my children, the importance of,
Heeding to Your word, as we abide within love.

Prayers and Praise in Poetic Phrase: Volume Four

For whom the Lord loveth he **correcteth**; **even** as a **father** the son in
whom he delighteth.
(Proverbs 3:12)

*C*hallenges confront them, from without and within.
*O*bstacles will hinder, when hearts give in to sin.
*R*emind my dear children, that they belong to You.
*R*estore their dedication, whether their sins be more or few.
*E*ven before discipline is necessity.
*C*onvince, by conviction, as they yield to You completely.
*T*each them to learn, from the cloud of witnesses.
*E*xercise their patience, that they may learn, what godly fitness is.
*T*ests of life will strengthen, as repentance is practised.
*H*eal that their actions may be pure; lest they pretend, like an actor or
actress.

*E*vents from the past can pollute.
*V*anities can deter the resolute.
*E*motions can mislead and hinder.
*N*evertheless, bless my children, in Jesus's name, to remain Christ
centered.

*F*aith will fuel their fellowship, with You heavenly Father.
*A*s they repent and believe, their past will cease to bother.
*T*hough they may struggle, to see beyond their flaws.
*H*elp them to receive, that Christ has borne them all.
*E*xalt and heal; lest they seek out earthly thrills, and ignore Your call.
*R*evive, in Jesus's name, as they are moved to repent, of all down falls.

*W*hen You look at us, You see the blood of Christ.
*H*elp my children see, the reality, that our redemption was highly priced.
*O*n Christ our sins were pored, for he became a curse.
*M*ade heirs, sons and daughters, according to chapter and verse.

For whom the Lord loveth he correcteth; even as a father the son in whom he ***delighteth***.
(Proverbs 3:12)

David was a man, after Your own heart.
Even as he fled, he surrendered every part.
Lions roared, but Danial did not worry.
In faith Issac blessed Jacob, though his vision was blurry.
Grace my children, to love You, with all of their might.
Heal; lest their past, hinders spiritual sight.
The cloud of many witnesses, can encourage and motivate.
Even as You direct my children, in what to love, and what to hate.
Help, in Jesus's name, as they seek and contemplate.

Happy is the man that findeth wisdom, and the man that getteth understanding.
(Proverbs 3:13)

Happiness is found, as we abide within Your love.
As we move by faith, we mature, by the grace thereof.
Perceiving their faith, in Mathew Chapter nine,
Palsy was healed, for Christ's glory would shine, as a sure sign.
Yokefellows, with Christ, in Jesus's name,let my children align.

Prayers for our Children

Happy is the man ***that findeth*** wisdom, and the man that getteth
understanding.
(Proverbs 3:13)

*T*he waters of grief, will flood their souls.
*H*appenstance can cripple, causing doubt to be bold.
*A*llow Your word to transform their minds,
*T*hat circumstances may not deceive, through erroneous paradigms.

*F*loods of fear will attach their faith,
*I*ncreasing the possibility, of actions you hate.
*N*evertheless, if they do not grow weary,
*D*irections, from Your word, will navigate clearly.
*E*ducate my children, as they cast cares upon You.
*T*each them to rest, within Christ, and continue to bare fruit.
*H*e has paid it all, and repentance, holy living, is their proof.

Happy is the man that findeth ***wisdom***, and the man that getteth
understanding.
(Proverbs 3:13)

*W*eary of trying, despair is real.
*I*f left to themselves, they will not heal.
*S*atisfy my children, for You are enough.
*D*irect their hearts, when they can't see Your love.
*O*ppositional voices will attempt to mislead.
*M*ake them able to see, that You alone, meet their need.

Happy is the man that findeth wisdom, and the man **that getteth**
understanding.
(Proverbs 3:13)

*T*heir is no understanding, outside of Christ.
*H*eavenly wisdom, is not by human device.
*A*s my children, seek for You, as precious gold,
*T*ransform and remold, their hearts, according to Your wisdom, in Jesus's name, manifold.

*G*race my children, in the mist of enemies.
*E*xperimentation, can wound a legacy.
*T*hey will be hated, without cause,
*T*hough they only live, for Your applause.
*E*ven as Christ was hated,
*T*heir walk will cause others to be aggravated.
*H*elp them to endure, in Jesus's name, for Christ will reward the consecrated.

Prayers and Praise in Poetic Phrase: Volume Four

Happy is the man that findeth wisdom, and the man that getteth
understanding.
(Proverbs 3:13)

*U*nited with You, through Christ, who paid the ultimate price,
*N*evertheless, there is no need to fear, for Your word is not mere advise.
*D*etermining the end from the beginning, You are God alone.
*E*ven in various trials, we are winning, for this earth is not home.
*R*emind them of Your prophet Moses, who sought no temporal riches.
*S*trategies given to Your people, informing them of which isn't; and which is.
*T*here is more to wisdom, than the accumulation of knowledge.
*A*ccording to the scripture, that is a recipe for prideful haulage.
*N*evertheless, grace my children to see,
*D*irections from You, provide health and stability.
*I*n and out of season, bless my children to decrease.
*N*avigate their hearts, even as they wait for release.
*G*rowing humbly, in Jesus's name, will increase their love, joy, and peace.

For the *merchandise* of it is *better* than the merchandise of silver, and
the gain therefore than fine gold.
(Proverbs 3:14)

*M*ake my children able, to buy clothing from Christ:
*E*ternal covering beyond earthly price.
*R*iches which will never see decay.
*C*hrist has abundant life, which never fades away.
*H*ands to the plow, without looking back,
*A*s they love You lord, even when under attack.
*N*o weapon formed against them, will never prevail.
*D*uring times of great persecution, there is peace, in the mist of hell.
I know You are able, to do these things and more,
*S*urpassing by the words You've given, for by them, You do restore.
*E*ven as You desire our victory, during peacetime and war.

*B*egging for acceptance, from this temporal world,
*E*ngenders to eternal fire, into which sinners shall be hurled.
*T*each my children, of the eternal bliss,
*T*hat entails suffering now, but will result in everlasting happiness.
*E*ven as they are tempted, to yield to compromise,
*R*einforce their ability, in Jesus's name, to resist Satan's lies.

For the merchandise of it is better *than* the merchandise of silver, and
the gain therefore than fine gold.
(Proverbs 3:14)

*T*his present suffering will not compare, to the glory that will be
revealed.
*H*eavenly Father, many do not care, that by Christ's stripes, we have
been healed.
*A*llow my children to see that eternity is at stake.
*N*ow is the preparation, in Jesus's name, for Christ's sake.

For the merchandise of it is better than the ***merchandise*** of ***silver***, and
the gain therefore than fine gold.
(Proverbs 3:14)

*M*orning brings new mercy, for You are love.
*E*ach second should be used to see You, for You are more than enough.
*R*eciting Your word, and taking heed,
*C*leanses of impurities, which seem to supply our need.
*H*indrances eclipse You, if we fail to yield.
*A*llowing You to reign, I'm matured and healed.
*N*ow a days, the enemy is not playing paddy cake.
*D*eception is the tool he uses; lest we remain awake.
I pray for my children; lest they are distracted.
*S*eeing the prosperity of the wicked, they may be attracted.
*E*quip them, with power, in Jesus's name; lest this world leaves them
negatively impacted.

*S*aying, "They need not depart; give ye them to eat."
*I*dentifying as "I Am", Christ supplied their meat.
*L*earning from Matthew chapter fourteen, for it testifies,
*V*erifying with Visualization that the Son supplies.
*E*ven as my children look to meet their need,
*R*eveal, Your provision, in Jesus's name, with spiritual percision; lest
they fall prey to greed.

For the merchandise of it is better than the merchandise of silver, and
the ***gain therefore than*** fine gold.
(Proverbs 3:14)

*G*race my children to desire heavenly wisdom, for ungodly forces are at
work.
*A*nd grace them to bow, here and now; lest they are prone to go
berserk.
*I*ncrease their dependence, for you alone can heal.
*N*avigate beyond earthy treasures, which have only a temporal appeal.

"*T*here were some who had indignation within themselves", in Mark
chapter fourteen.
*H*aving an alabaster box of ointment, she poured, massaged, and
cleaned.
*E*veryone may not understand, their show of appreciation.
*R*umors may demean their acts of service, or application.
*E*quip them by Your Spirit, to honor as You've called.
*F*or their alabaster box, is theirs to give away or be hauled.
*O*rdering their steps, according to Your word,
*R*evives and strengthens, and keeps their hearts stirred.
*E*levate their thinking, in Jesus's name; lest Your methods seem absurd.

*T*hrough wisdom, You created all.
*H*elp my children, to walk within Your call.
*A*s they see, the necessity thereof,
*N*evertheless, they will be blessed, as they apply wisdom, within love.

For the merchandise of it is better than the merchandise of silver, and
the gain therefore than ***fine*** gold.
(Proverbs 3:14)

*F*inding buried treasure, requires a search.
*I*ncrease my children's desire, to put in spiritual work.
*N*ow, before the storm, that they may be prepared.
*E*quip them by Your Spirit; lest by this world they are ensnared.

Prayers and Praise in Poetic Phrase: Volume Four

For the merchandise of it is better than the merchandise of silver, and
the gain therefore than fine **gold**.
(Proverbs 3:14)

Grace my children to see their worth, within Your biblical pages.
Order their steps and heal whelps, gained from various stages.
Let the revelation of Christ distill.
Disciple, in Jesus's name, as my children repent, within Your will.

She is **more precious** than rubies: and all the things thou canst desire
are not to be compared unto her.
(Proverbs 3:15)

Motivate my children to seek Your ways.
Order their steps, as Your wisdom is obeyed.
Remind them to search, Your word, for understanding.
Eternal life is within Christ, in Jesus's name, bless their comprehending.

Placing Your word, above all else, is wisdom.
Reward is found, in Christ, beyond this worldly system.
Even as the wicked seem to prosper,
Counter the wiles, which hinder the gospel.
I ask that You'd grace my children to decrease,
Otherwise, they violate Your will and their peace.
Using Your word as their guide,
Strength will be found, in Jesus's name, as self is denied.

She is more precious **than rubies**: and all the **things** thou canst desire
are not to be compared unto her.
(Proverbs 3:15)

The wisdom of this world is foolishness to You.
Help my children to align with Your view.
Allow them to see the necessity, for the mind of Christ.
Nearsightedness and spiritual obesity, is not an acceptable living
sacrifice.

Reveal the wisdom of Your Spirit, for this world is not the home, of the
believer.
Useless is spiritual speech, if their life is ruled, by the deceiver.
Bless my children with the will to yield, totally to You.
In Christ, Your will is fulfilled, as they repent and follow through.
Ephesians chapter one, verse three,
Supports the blessings of the believer, spiritually.

The way to destruction is broad; the way to life is narrow.
Help my children to see through facades, that they can discern between
bone and marrow.
In all things bless them to see, that Jesus is their rest,
Not settling for temporal, but live by what Christ says is best.
Grace my children, in Jesus's name, to desire more of You.
Satisfy, their entire being, as they repent, as they have been called to.

Prayers for our Children

She is more precious than rubies: and all the things **thou canst desire**
are not to be compared unto her.
(Proverbs 3:15)

*T*asting and seeing that You are good,
*H*earing and doing, as Jesus would,
*O*btains the blessing of eternal life,
*U*nderstanding, that repentance, is evidence, of true trust in Christ.

*C*hrist did not desire to be served, but to serve,
*A*nd offer his life, as he took what we deserved,
*N*eeds will plead to be heard,
*S*triving and competing, with Your holy word.
*T*each my children, in Jesus's name, that Your Spirit may be referred.

*D*esires of the flesh contradict Your Spirit.
*E*ven good deeds alone, are not necessarily, biblically coherent.
*S*how my children, Your plan for them.
I ask that Your ways and their will become synonym.
*R*emind them that Christ has final say.
*E*vidence is repentance, grace them to turn, in Jesus's name.

She is more precious than rubies: and all the things thou canst desire
are not to be **compared** unto her.
(Proverbs 3:15)

*C*ertainly, this present suffering does not compare,
*O*bstacles and weapons remain, and seem, at times, unfair.
*M*an shall not live by bread alone, but it is necessary.
*P*repare my children, as they seek for a home, which is not temporary.
*A*s the children of Israel stood before a terrible mountain,
*R*ebuked; lest they touched it, blood would pour, like a fountain.
*E*ven to whom much is given, much is required,
*D*irect them, in Jesus's name, as Christ is their desire.

She is more precious than rubies: and all the things thou canst desire
are not to be compared ***unto*** her.
(Proverbs 3:15)

Using knowledge appropriately, is wise.
No understanding: will diminish territory and size.
Teach me to teach my children: well,
On purpose, by example, in Jesus's name; lest their flesh prevails.

Length of days is in her right hand; and in her left hand riches and honor
(Proverbs 3:16)

Long life is promised to followers of Christ,
External, to be exact, for Jesus gave up his life.
Not that we were worthy, for we were not.
Grace through faith, for his blood removes every blot.
The proof is repentance, a change of lifestyle.
Holiness is the evidence. In Jesus's name, help my child.

Prayers and Praise in Poetic Phrase: Volume Four

Length of ***days*** is in her ***right*** hand; and in her left hand riches and
honor
(Proverbs 3:16)

Discipleship, is godly wisdom in practise.
As Christ is made Lord, surrender is active.
You are able to perform any task.
Sincerely, bless my children, in Jesus's name, to live before You,
unmasked.

Righteous living, will leave one lacking.
Increasingly good deeds, are set on a foundation, that is cracking.
Gifts of praise and so called worship, unless Jesus is Lord,
Have no eternal baring, one must repent and unify with Christ, in one
accord.
Teach my Children, in Jesus's name, to surrender all, without shame.

Length of days is in her right **hand**; and in her **left hand** riches and honor
(Proverbs 3:16)

Hold my children, within the palm of Your hand.
And protect them, within this wicked land.
Now more than ever, bless them to see, Christ as a need.
Direct, by Your Spirit, in Jesus's name, I plead.

Let Your word place a desire within their heart.
Even, a desire to surrender, to Christ, every, single part.
For tomorrow is not promised, today is the day.
Touch my children, for Your glory, in Jesus's name, that they may
continue, within Your way.

Heavenly citizen, really?
Actions betray, as they look so silly.
Nevertheless, convict for Your glory.
Direct my children, in Jesus's name, for their repentance is mandatory.

Length of days is in her right hand; and in her left hand **riches** and **honor**
(Proverbs 3:16)

Riches, of the kingdom, are beyond earthly price.
In Christ, they are freely given, because of his sacrifice.
Challenges of life: failures, successes, and external judgments,
Have hindered the clarity of my children's spiritual descent.
Ease their hearts, as they seek Your face.
Satisfy their concerns, in Jesus's name, as they live, a life of repentance,
by Your grace.

Heavenly Father, the world honors what You hate.
Overcomers are on Your side, not pron to vacillate.
Navigate the motives of their heart, for at times, they are tempted to
veer.
Observing this world, my children may, choose to emotionally steer.
Refine and realign, in Jesus's name, that they may be moved by godly
fear.

Her **ways** are ways of pleasantness, and all her paths are peace
(Proverbs 3:17)

Wisdom which comes from You, enhances my children's view.
Allowing eternal access to the power which flows from You.
Yesterday is gone, Christ calls for repentance today.
Solely, all riches are through Jesus, grace my children, in Jesus's name,
to surrender and obey.

Prayers for our Children

Her ways are **ways** of pleasantness, and all her paths are peace
(Proverbs 3:17)

When my children abide within You, their peace is steady and sure.
As they deny themselves, You reprove, and grace motives to be pure.
Yielding to emotions, will only lead to loss.
Satisfy, my children, in Jesus's name, as the seek to take up their cross.

Her ways are ways of **pleasantness**, and all her paths are peace
(Proverbs 3:17)

Placing trust within themselves, and what they think is correct,
Leaves my children lacking, as Your word they disrespect.
Even if sincerity, is the place from which they come,
At the end of their attempts, sadly the benefit, is little to none.
Sadducees and Pharisees thought themselves very clever.
And Jesus sharply rebuked, "You are of your father the devil."
Not that their intentions, were to have such a testimony.
The act of being godly, within self, isn't real, but phoney.
Not unlike the brood of vipers, who claimed to walk upright,
Emotions take the lead, when self seeks to walk by sight.
Sincerely, contrariwise, bless my children to grow.
Securely, within the grace and knowledge of Jesus Christ, as they
discard excess cargo.

Her ways are ways of pleasantness, and all her **paths** are peace
(Proverbs 3:17)

Practising wisdom, is a challenge to the flesh.
According to biblical text, the flesh and the Spirit, do not mesh.
Teach my children the root, of emotional reactions.
Heal, for wounds from the past, can be come a distraction.
Secure their souls, in Jesus's name; lest they be drawn to various attractions.

Her ways are ways of pleasantness, and all her paths are **peace**
(Proverbs 3:17)

Practising wisdom, which comes from You,
Edifies the recipient, neighbors, and bystanders too.
As my children decrease, in obedience to Christ.
Challenges will increase, for the flesh hates sacrifice.
Extinguish internal duality, double mindedness, in Jesus's name; lest their loyalty is sliced.

She is a **tree** of **life** to them that lay hold upon her: and happy is every one that retaineth her.
(Proverbs 3:18)

The wisdom You provide, will groom them.
Renew their minds, and bloom them.
Empower my children to grow, in Jesus's name.
Even as they seek to know You, without shame.

Lord, grace my children, to abide within Your vine.
Increase their hunger and thirst,as their hearts are refined.
For true wisdom comes from You,
Even understanding, from an eternal biblical view.

Prayers and Praise in Poetic Phrase

She is a tree of life to ***them that*** lay hold upon her: and happy is every
one that retaineth her.
(Proverbs 3:18)

*T*here is no guarantee of salvation, one must endure til the end.
*H*eavenly obedience, within repentance, confirms that Christ is a friend.
*E*agerness is good, but endurance is better.
*M*aking one's calling and election sure, for Christ has freed, from
worldly fetters.

*T*he process of wisdom requires patience, for You work within Your
timing.
*H*elp my children this very hour; lest they fail, to keep their light shining.
*A*s they cut off every sin, and repent of iniquity,
*T*each them, that Christ dwells within, in Jesus's name, ubiquity.

She is a tree of life to them that lay ***hold upon*** her: and happy is every
one that retaineth her.
(Proverbs 3:18)

*H*elp my children to persevere, though their faith be tested.
*O*bserving You, grace them to increase, and remain Christ centered and
rested.
*L*oving You heavenly Father, with all of their heart,
*D*emonstrates, as their loves and hates, align with You, their secret,
hidden parts.

*U*nderstanding that Your law is best, will help them be faithful.
*P*ractising prayer, casting cares upon You, display that they are grateful.
*O*pportunities to stray, will avail multiple times a day.
*N*evertheless, grace my children, in Jesus's name, to live within Your
holy way.

She is a tree of life to them that lay hold upon her: and **happy** is **every**
one that retaineth her.
(Proverbs 3:18)

*H*aving an eternal perspective, and sowing to that end,
*A*llows Your word to be effective, and results in tremendous dividends.
*P*lace within my children a hunger, for Your righteousness, let them thirst.
*P*lace within a will to serve You, as they surrender, to chapter and verse.
*Y*okefellow with Christ, in Jesus's name, much richer; not poorer, much better; not worse.

*E*veryday the choice is made, to walk within, or out of Christ.
*V*anities compete with wisdom, and are extremely over priced.
*E*mpower my children, to make whatever the sacrifice.
*R*edeeming their precious time, for mere effects of the flesh, are worthless and imprecise.
*Y*ou satisfy, grace my children, in Jesus's name, to choose eternal paradise.

She is a tree of life to them that lay hold upon her: and happy is every
one *that* retaineth her.
(Proverbs 3:18)

*T*each my children, to choose wisdom more and more.
*H*elp them view eternal life, as something worth living for.
*A*s this world becomes worse, and iniquity abounds,
*T*ransform their paradigms, in Jesus's name, as they cast ungodly imaginations down.

Prayers for our Children

She is a tree of life to them that lay hold upon her: and happy is every
one that *retaineth* her.
(Proverbs 3:18)

*R*eveal their need, to contend for the faith.
*E*motions mislead, for they will vacillate.
*T*each them the wisdom, which comes from above.
*A*nd allow them to maneuver within the realm of love.
*I*n Christ they will live, move, and have their being.
*N*evertheless, as they repent of worldly things.
*E*ven as a new born babe, bless them to desire Your word.
*T*each them to thirst, in Jesus's name; lease hope is deferred.

The *Lord* by *wisdom hath* founded the earth; by understanding hath he
established the heavens
(Proverbs 3:19)

*L*ord, I thank You for an opportunity, to know Your ways.
*O*therwise, I'd have no choice, but to remain, within a worldly phase.
*R*emind my children, that Your will is best.
*D*irect, in Jesus's name, through every trial and test.

*W*alking in obedience, to our Saviour, is wisdom indeed.
*I*ncreasing goodness and mercy, is there to meet the need.
*S*atisfy, my children, as they keep Christ's commands.
*D*ecrease their desire, to seek Your hand.
*O*bserving Your love, let them seek Your face.
*M*ay they seek to please Your heart, in Jesus's name, as they live, by
Your grace.

*H*eavenly Father, grace my children, to desire, Your will, to be done.
*A*lso transform, as they admire, and thirst, for more, of Your Son.
*T*each them that His words, are Spirit and life.
*H*eal them as they are willing, in Jesus's name, to surrender, and self
sacrifice.

The Lord by wisdom hath ***founded*** the earth; by understanding hath he established the heavens

(Proverbs 3:19)

Form the core of their personality, as they seek after Christ.
Observing His every word, they'll be strengthen for self sacrifice.
Use their daily situations, to draw them closer still.
Navigate as they surrender, wholeheartedly, to Your will.
Direct them to not conform, to temptation from without or within.
Even when they feel alone, embrace, as they repent of sin.
Disciple my children, in Jesus's name, for this world is not a friend.

The Lord by wisdom hath founded the ***earth***; by understanding hath he established the heavens

(Proverbs 3:19)

Evidence of Your existence, can be found in any place.
And the wonders You have made, testify of Your embrace.
Remind my children of Your love, if they are ever faced, with doubtfulness.
Touch their hearts, for You are faithful, even as Your chosen, experience this.
Heal their broken heart, in Jesus's name, as Your Son they kiss.

Prayers and Praise In Poetic Phrase: Volume Four

The Lord by wisdom hath founded the earth; by **understanding hath** he
established the heavens
(Proverbs 3:19)

*Un*less You grant the ability, for their eyes to see.
No light can penetrate, their hearts will darken, spiritually.
Do you have the power to change a heart,
*Ev*en if the past, has torn it apart?
*Re*build, for my children, have been broken.
*St*art with their foundation, for Your Son has spoken.
*Te*ach them to fear You, for therein is love.
*An*d satisfy, fortify, that they may know, that You are enough.
No one will deny, as they stand before You.
*Di*rect, for Christ is coming, to give all their due.
In and out of season, grace them to thirst.
*Na*vigate their desires, towards Your chapters and verse.
*Gr*ace them with understanding, in Jesus's name; lest they behave even
worst.

*He*al, for my child's understanding, has been molested,
*At*tacked and distorted, their innocence has been arrested.
*Ta*re down the walls, which have been built, within, offense.
*He*al, for their fall has created, direr emotional consequence.

The Lord by wisdom hath founded the earth; by understanding hath he
established the heavens
(Proverbs 3:19)

*E*motions will definitely mislead, if they are allowed.
*S*ticks and stones will bruise, as they follow the crowd.
*T*each my children to be led, by Your words alone.
*A*nd that character isn't always bred, within a "happy home".
*B*less my children to be a aware of what they cannot change.
*L*ove can conquer all, if Christ is allowed to rearrange.
I've made mistakes which have hindered.
*S*atisfy and purify, as they remain surrendered.
*H*eavenly Father, these things I ask, in Jesus's name.
*E*stablish their hearts, by Your grace; lest they be ashamed.
*D*isciple, as they seek to abhor the vain.

The Lord by wisdom hath founded the earth; by understanding hath he
established the ***heavens***
(Proverbs 3:19)

*H*eaven and earth are stable, filled with consistency.
*E*ven as the seasons change, there is a certain, certainty.
*A*llow my children to see, the beauty they display.
*V*isions of heaven and earth, which broadcast glory everyday.
*E*ven as they sometimes struggle, to walk obediently.
*N*evertheless, the day will come, that they must be judged before Thee.
*S*et them apart, as they surrender their hearts, in Jesus's name, for Your
glory.

Prayers for our Children

By his **knowledge** the depths are broken up, and the clouds drop down
the dew.
(Proverbs 3:20)

Knowledge alone, does not satisfy.
No action applied, means you disqualify.
Observing the mistakes, of others, we will learn and grow.
Wisdom is like the wings of an eagle, which enable us to soar, as we
obey what we know.
Learning from the cloud of witnesses, from the old testament and new.
Even as we surrender, education will ensue.
Daily devotional time, would extremely benefit.
Grace my children, with a desire, to manage and handle it.
Empower, in Jesus's name; lest they faint, and prove illegitimate.

By his knowledge the **depths** are **broken** up, and the clouds drop down
the dew.
(Proverbs 3:20)

Deeply afraid, to lose their position,
Educated priests and elders sought to kill Jesus, for he threatened their
ambition.
Pontius Pilate witnessed something suspicious in the air.
Though he could have intervened, he did not want to lose his chair.
Heal my children, though their wounds run deep.
Sanctify their desires, in Jesus's name, for they shall sow what they
reap.

Bowing in submission, as I repent of sin,
Removes the strength of strongholds, and brings fear's rule to an end.
Observing my lifestyle, as I walk within your light,
Keeps me, for Your glory, and inspires others, to endure the fight.
Even as my children, seek their independence,
Nourish, by Your word, in Jesus's name, as they submit, in full
attendance.

By his knowledge the depths are broken up, and the ***clouds drop down***
the dew.
(Proverbs 3:20)

*C*louds carry water, which sustains all.
*L*ike blessings, there is a process, before the rain falls.
*O*ur of order, out of step, with Your plans,
*U*nlearned individuals, who deny Your commands,
*D*o not secure Your favor, but wrath is in store.
*S*aturate my Children, in Jesus name, as they seek You more and more.

*D*rain my children, of all selfishness, for Christ calls for self denial.
*R*eigning, by Your Spirit, according to Your word, combats the enemy's
wiles.
*O*pen the eyes of their understanding, that they may see the value,
*P*ouring from the wounds of Christ, in Jesus's name, as they humbly bow
too.

*D*oubt can hinder obedience, grant the increase of their faith.
*O*bserving the winds and waves, they may become discouraged, during
their wait.
*W*itnesses have gone before, from the old testament and new.
*N*arrow is the way, in Jesus's name, bless my children, to maintain, a
heavenly view.

My son, let not ***them depart from*** thine eyes: keep sound wisdom and discretion:
(Proverbs 3:21)

*T*he wisdom, understanding, and knowledge You give, is of eternal benefit.
*H*ealing results from them, which is indiscriminant.
*E*mpower my children, as they humbly, submit to You.
*M*aking sure their call, in Jesus's name, though their peers fall; You can strengthen and renew.

*D*eparting from Your wisdom, is a foolish thing to do.
*E*ven temporal success, does not profit without You.
*P*repare my children, for Christ's return, which could happen any day.
*A*nd if Christ should tarry, their last breath could escape, their delicate airway.
*R*emind my children, to endure until the end.
*T*o be weary, in well doing, could lead a soul, to sin.

*F*ortify their faith, as they seek to keep Christ's commands.
*R*emind them of self denial, and carrying their cross, as He demands.
*O*thers will give heed to lying: seducing spirits.
*M*ake my children, able to see, beyond visible appearance.

My son, let not them depart from ***thine eyes***: ***keep*** sound wisdom and discretion:
(Proverbs 3:21)

*T*here is only one, they should seek to please.
*H*aving an audience, of the Son, is enough, as they believe.
I pray that their actions, confirm their faith.
*N*avigating the narrow way, for the reward, is worth the wait.
*E*ncourage their heart, in Jesus's name, as they seek to walk the straight.

*E*vil will deceive, if care isn't taken.
*Y*ou will keep Your children, for You have never forsaken.
*E*ven as they seek, to meditate upon Your word,
*S*anctify and satisfy, in Jesus's name, as they obey, what they have heard.

*K*ept by Your Spirit, for Christ has paid the cost.
*E*ven if they do well, it's useless without the cross.
*E*nlighten their souls, and reveal this actuality:
*P*ractising perfection is possible, for Christ's died, after keeping every technicality.

My son, let not them depart from thine eyes: keep ***sound wisdom*** and discretion:
(Proverbs 3:21)

*S*easons change, but Your word, remains the same.
*O*pposing viewpoints, ungodly wiles, will attempt to take the reins.
*U*nable to defeat the faithful, where Christ is preeminent,
*N*evertheless, they deceive the ungrateful, who contend with the diligent.
*D*irect my Children, in Jesus's name, for Christ's return is imminent.

*W*orldly treasures call, and feel so satisfying.
*I*ncreasingly many fall, for they will give heed to lying.
*S*trengthen my children, as they lay aside every weight.
*D*irect their hearts to self denial, as they seek, to walk the straight.
*O*btaining wisdom through Christ, eternal riches abound.
*M*ade heirs with You, and joint heirs with Your Son: ingrafted renown.

55

My son, let not them depart from thine eyes: keep sound wisdom and
discretion:
(Proverbs 3:21)

*D*iscretion can keep them, as they walk, within Your ways.
*I*ncreasingly, it is needful, for we are in the last days.
*S*ocietal norms contradict, Your holy mind,
*C*onforming them, to synonyms, which pervert, Your purpose and design.
*R*evive a godly hunger, which could only come from You.
*E*mpower them to endure, as they abide within Your truth.
*T*each them to present themselves, as a living sacrifice.
*I*ncrease within their hearts, as they decrease, for the sake of Christ.
*O*bserving Your word, increases their discretion.
*N*evertheless, as they obey, in Jesus's name, refreshen.

So ***shall they*** be ***life*** unto thy soul, and grace to thy neck.
(Proverbs 3:22)

*S*overeign, heavenly, Father, You have given us Your Son.
*H*e is the mediator, who makes Your children, and You one.
*A*llow my children to understand, that Christ is the only way.
*L*et resurrection power, flow through them, as they obey.
*L*ead them to repentance, in Jesus's name; lest they fall by the way.

*T*he words of Christ, are Spirit and life, and draw us to You, heavenly Father.
*H*elp my children to see, their necessity, though at times, His speech seems to bother.
*E*ven when bitter, they lead to life, and form His mind within us.
*Y*ou gave Your Word, which is our Christ, which justifies and defends us.

*L*ife free, from the rule of depression, is within Christ.
*I*n Him is love, joy, and peace, as we sacrifice.
*F*ortify the resolve of my children, as they seek His favor.
*E*ven as He led by example, as He served, as our Savior.

So shall they be life *unto* thy *soul*, and *grace* to thy neck.
(Proverbs 3:22)

Understanding that Christ is key, to all things good.
No sane person, with this knowledge, would despise wormwood.
Towards the Saviour, move my children, they know not what's best.
Open their eyes, in Jesus's name, as they strive, to enter His rest.

Solutions claim to help, but do not atone, or compensate.
Only one can justify, Christ alone has borne sin's weight.
Use the pains of this world, to draw my children closer.
Lead by Your Spirit, in Jesus's name; lest their hearts roller coaster.

Goodness and mercy, should shape my Child.
Renew their strength; lest they pursue the wild.
As they consider, their path of life,
Confusion will attempt, to increase their strife.
Empower, in Jesus's name, as Your words cut flesh, like a knife.

Prayers and Praise in Poetic Phrase: Volume Four

So shall they be life unto thy soul, and grace to thy *neck*.
(Proverbs 3:22)

Necklaces of sorrow and bitterness, will cripple if allowed.
Emotions will cause, much more than this, especially if led by the crowd.
Convince my children that You are good, as they taste You day by day.
Keep them within Your word, in Jesus's name, as they seek to learn Your
way.

Then shall thou walk in thy way safely, and thy foot shall not stumble.
(Proverbs 3:23)

They will walk in the way safely, if they take heed to Christ.
He is alpha and omega, the way, truth, and life.
Educate my children, within Your ways.
Nevertheless, as they abide and rest, in Jesus's name, even through difficult phase.

Separating themselves, from every unclean thing,
Hinders strongholds, and the rule of earthly kings.
As my children heed the words of Christ,
Love will keep their hearts, from stronghold and heist.
Lead my children, in Jesus's name, as they rest within Christ's sacrifice.

Though Christ has died, for the sins of every one,
Healing will not be found, for each daughter and son.
Only those who surrender, wholeheartedly
Undergo transformation, which leads to true intimacy.

Then shall thou *walk* in thy way *safely*, and thy foot shall not stumble.
(Proverbs 3:23)

Within Christ goodness and mercy, will follow each day of life.
All out battle will ensue, for between the flesh and the Spirit is strife.
Lust and the word, are mortal enemies.
Keep my children, in Jesus's name, as they fight, within victory.

Security within Christ, is the best promise man has ever seen.
As my children look to Your word, and rest within John, three, sixteen.
Few will find the way, for many will not submit.
Even some will claim a title, with no eternal benefit.
Let love persevere, for the godly will suffer persecution.
You are able to keep my child, in Jesus's name, for within Christ, is the solution.

Then shall thou walk in thy way safely, and thy *foot* shall not stumble.
(Proverbs 3:23)

*F*ortify the foundation, of my child's identity.
*O*therwise, they will fall like, rain from a tree.
*O*pen wide their eyes, that they might see their need.
*T*ouch my child's understanding, in Jesus's name; lest they operate out of greed.

Then shall thou walk in thy way safely, and thy foot *shall* not stumble.
(Proverbs 3:23)

*S*atisfy my children, as they seek to follow Christ.
*H*elp them realize, that this world is overpriced.
*A*lthough in appearance, they move against the grain,
*L*ove must motivate, as they walk, in Jesus's name.
*L*ead them by Your Spirit; lest they make their moves in vain.
Prayers for our Children

Then shall thou walk in thy way safely, and thy foot shall not *stumble*.
(Proverbs 3:23)

*S*trategies from the enemy, will confuse the naive.
*T*rials and temptation, will cause many to disbelieve.
*U*sing various tools, You make Your children better.
*M*ake my children stronger, than their current chain and fetter.
*B*less them to cleave to Christ with all of their heart.
*L*ove has a way of reaching every part.
*E*ven as they yield and declare, "How Great Thou Art!"

When thou liest down, thou shall not be afraid: yea, thou shall lie down,
and thy sleep shall be sweet.
(Proverbs 3:24)

While Martha had complaints, Mary was at rest.
Healing results from obeying Christ, as within him, we nest.
Even when others attack, for they do not understand,
Nevertheless, saturate my children, in Jesus's name, for Your kingdom is at hand.

The lions did not touch Daniel, though they were kept hungry.
He rested, in their presence, as an owl, safe within a pine tree.
Opposition will persecute my children, as they follow the King of Kings.
Undermine the enemy's strategies, in Jesus's name; lest they are misled by temporal things.

Lying in the mist of a storm, our Savior was sound asleep.
In concern for their very lives, they awoke Christ, whose flesh was bound within sleep.
Even though the Son was present, the disciples welcomed fear.
Save my children from emotions, which would cause their hearts to veer.
Teach them to walk by faith, in Jesus's name, as they sincerely persevere.

When thou liest **down, thou** shall not be afraid: yea, thou shall lie down,
and thy sleep shall be sweet.
(Proverbs 3:24)

Direct my children, during highs and lows.
Offence can come, from friends or foes.
Within Christ, there is a Spirit, of power and love.
Nourish my child, in Jesus's name, within the peace thereof.

There is no fear in Love, for perfect love casts out fear.
Hardened hearts are susceptible, to wiles within the atmosphere.
Observing Christ's forgiveness, even as he hung upon a tree.
Upholding His example, in Jesus's name, bless my children to agree, and move accordingly.

When thou liest down, thou **shall** not be afraid: yea, thou shall lie down,
and thy sleep shall be sweet.
(Proverbs 3:24)

Sin will increase doubt and fear, if repentance is nonexistent.
Healing by His stripes, and the practise of sin, is inconsistent.
As my children deny themselves, take up their cross, and follow Christ,
Love will be perfected, otherwise their hearts will ice.
Lead them, in Jesus's name, as they present themselves, as a living sacrifice.

Prayers and Praise in Poetic Phrase: Volume Four

When thou liest down, thou shall not be **afraid**: yea, **thou shall** lie
down, and thy sleep shall be sweet.
(Proverbs 3:24)

Allow my children to rest, within what Christ has done.
Fortify their commitment, as they surrender to Your Son.
Remind them that repentance, is necessity.
And that a proof of salvation, is godly charity.
In Christ, is no fear of earthly consequence.
Disciple, for Your glory, in Jesus's name: godly evidence; lest before
Christ, they are ashamed.

Thank You for the promises, that Christ has given.
Heal my children, as they allow Your word, to direct their living.
Open their eyes and ears unto You, for without they are blind.
Unleash their desire, for Your hunger and fire, instead of fear, bless
them with a sound mind.

So much stimuli, makes it difficult to focus.
Hell seeks to devour, like a field of hungry locus.
Allow them to breathe, and not suffocate.
Lead by Your Spirit, as they walk by faith;
Lest they are deceived, by erroneous debate.

When thou liest down, thou shall not be afraid: yea, thou shall lie **down**,
and thy **sleep shall** be sweet.
(Proverbs 3:24)

Decrease their desire, to control all things.
Offer them position, beneath the shadow of Your wings.
Whenever they are tempted, to stress and depress,
Navigate, in Jesus's name, as they make Christ their rest.

Sometimes the bed could be, a place of restlessness.
Letting go of the days concerns, would create a peaceful rest.
Every wile, test, and trial is to be placed, within Your care.
Empower my child, to cast their cares upon You, and leave their burdens there.
Place peace, love, and joy, in Jesus's name, within, that they might share.

Some Seasons of struggle, seem to have no end.
Heavenly Father, Your love, at times, is hidden beneath disruptive trends.
Allow my children faith, as they cling onto Your words.
Let them not be pulled away, by wicked, worldly herds.
Let them feel Your embrace, as their spirit man is stirred.

When thou liest down, thou shall not be afraid: yea, thou shall lie down,
and thy sleep shall be **sweet**.
(Proverbs 3:24)

Satisfying the senses, as You are enjoyed,
Without exception, You comfort my wounds, and fill every void.
Even the rebukes and reproofs, will amount to a glorious end.
Enlighten my children with knowledge; lest without repentance, they attempt to call You friend.
Transform their desires and increase holy fire, in Jesus's name, amend.

Be not *afraid* of *sudden* fear, neither of the desolation of the wicked,
when it cometh.
(Proverbs 3:25)

Allowing fear, is no choice for the believer.
For Jesus has overcome, sin and the deceiver.
Raised us up together, with Christ, in heavenly places,
And in the mist of the storm, peace, can be our holy oasis.
I ask that You'd teach, my children to sow,
Deeply into the things of Your Spirit, that they may mature and grow.

Sharp turns occur, so one must be ready.
Understanding can ensure, that my children, are secure and steady.
Decrease their dependence, on what they see.
Decrease their pride, and self sufficiency.
Eating and drinking of Christ, strengthens faith to persevere.
Nevertheless, put in place, by your grace, an established godly base, to
relieve sudden fear.

Be not afraid of sudden *fear*, *neither* of the desolation of the wicked,
when it cometh.
(Proverbs 3:25)

Fear has torment, which will hinder.
Each day, by Your grace, bless my children to surrender.
And grant them the ability to abound, even within drought.
Renewal and fuel dwell, in Jesus's name, without fear and doubt.

Navigation is needed, for mazes abound.
Emotions heeded, impede spiritual ground.
I pray that You increase their faith,
That they may mature, enough to wait.
Help them to be happy, as they rejoice.
Even as You reveal, that victory is a choice.
Reserved for those, who are obiedaint to Your holy voice.

Be not afraid of sudden fear, neither of the **desolation** of the **wicked**, when it cometh.

(Proverbs 3:25)

Direction from Christ is not always a breeze.
Educations, of the Spirit, may bring us to our knees.
Struggle will ensue, for we are at war.
Orders from above, shake our hearts to the core.
Let love for You, be the reason for change.
As they seek to prescribe, to what You've prearranged.
There may be times, that care will grip them.
I know that fear will seek to sift and whip them.
Only You will save, as they deny self,
Navigate, with their cross, and follow Christ, to their death.

Witnesses attest to the peace You provide.
In faith, through the fire, the three Hebrews were safely kept inside.
Confusion from a king, kept David moving.
Kissed by goodness and mercy, the future king, kept prospering and improving.
Even as they were, in the mist of a deadly storm,
Disciples found Jesus sleeping, in peace, without alarm.

Prayers and Praise in Poetic Phrase: Volume Four

Be not afraid of sudden fear, neither of the desolation of the wicked,
                          when it cometh.
(Proverbs 3:25)

When Judas came with his kiss, Christ understood.
Hell plots for our demise; You work all things for our good.
Even when the enemy seems to have the upper hand.
Nevertheless, grace my children to embrace Your truth, that they may understand.

Be not afraid of sudden fear, neither of the desolation of the wicked,
when it ***cometh***.
(Proverbs 3:25)

Considering first John, verse eighteen, there is no fear in love.
Obstacles and dramatic scenes, can not disrupt the peace thereof.
Multiply Your love, as they abide within Your truth.
Educate them within Your ways, for Your words are resolute.
Teach them to truth You, with there whole heart.
Help them rest, in Jesus's name, and live a life, set apart.

For the ***Lord shall*** be thy confidence, and shall keep thy foot from being
taken.
(Proverbs 3:26)

Lead my children, as they keep confidence within You.
Obtaining and gaining godly wisdom, as they live as Christ has called
them to.
Remind them that they, have been bought with a price.
Disciple, in Jesus's name, as they present themselves, as a living
sacrifice.

Saying a prayer is not following Christ.
Hearing the word without repentance: useless sacrifice.
As my children move throughout their day, lions and wolves view them
as prey,
Lustful, hidden figures and emotional triggers, will seek to have their
way.
Lead my precious children, in Jesus's name; lest Christ's words are
betrayed.

For the Lord shall be thy ***confidence***, and shall keep thy foot from being taken.
(Proverbs 3:26)

Confidence in man is a curse, for who is like You Lord.
Observing holy chapter and verse, its a gamble no one can afford.
No love can compare, to the comfort You provide.
Faithful to Your promise, it flows out to others, from the inside.
In Your presence is the fullness of joy, and pleasures forevermore.
Decrease they do their peace, as they depend on earthly reservoirs.
Empower my children to trust, You with their whole heart.
Nevertheless, let Your word get drilled in, as they surrender every part.
Confessing and decreeing means little, if its only words.
Equip my children for action, in Jesus's name; lest they follow ungodly herds.

For the Lord shall be thy confidence, and ***shall*** keep thy foot from being taken.
(Proverbs 3:26)

Shouting prayers and praise mean nothing, if my children do not repent.
Help them to understand, it's required for covenant.
As my children keep Christ's commands, their sin is forgiven.
Love is gentle yet reprimands, it's that Christ-centered living.
Lord, in Jesus's name, grace them to trust and walk it out, within thanks giving.

Prayers of our Children

For the Lord shall be thy confidence, and shall **keep** thy **foot** from being taken**.**

*K*ept, for Christ has intervened and overcome.
*E*nemies of the cross have challenged, but have been made blind and dumb.
*E*motional responses produce the same result.
*P*repare my children, in Jesus's name, mature them to a spiritual adult.

*F*ortify my child, with the gospel truth.
*O*ffenders cause as much pain, as a broken tooth.
*O*ffenses will come, from without and within.
*T*ransform, in Jesus's name, as my child repents of sin.

For the Lord shall be thy confidence, and shall keep thy foot *from being taken.*
(Proverbs 3:26)

*F*aith without works is certainly dead.
*R*evive and Strengthen, as my children, obey what Christ said.
*O*bserving Your word,at times, can be a chore.
*M*anifest Your glory, in Jesus's name, as they seek You more.

*B*lessings abound for the faithful,
*E*ven to the disciplined and grateful.
*I*ncrease the desires of my children Lord.
*N*evertheless, grace them to surrender, across the board.
*G*rant, in Jesus's name, them Your favor, as they seek eternal glory and reward.

*T*his world will misuse, and abuse, with little, to no benefit.
*A*nd take all you have, still daring you to quit.
*K*eep my children safe, within Your loving arms.
*E*nemies plot with weapons, by which they seek to harm.
*N*evertheless, in Jesus's name, schemes may be felt, yet will all be disarmed.

Withhold not **good** from them to whom it is due, when it is in the
power of thine hand to do it.
(Proverbs 3:27)

When my children, are in position to help.
It may be tempting, to think of self.
Teach them, to act out of love.
Help them to understand, their portion thereof.
Heal wounds of the past, from when they were mistreated.
Order Your Ointment, of the Spirit, to aide where it is needed.
Let Your glory manifest, as they walk the straight.
Decrease is necessity, in Jesus's name, saturate.

Grace my children to look, beyond evil devices.
Opposition cuts their heart, as a knife, an apple, into slices.
Opportunities to take vengeance, will be present.
Direct, as my child rejects, the emotions of an adolescent.

Prayers and Praise in Poetic Phrase: Volume Four

Withhold not good **from them** to whom it is due, when it is in the power
of thine hand to do it.
(Proverbs 3:27)

Flaws seem much greater, than Christ commands.
Renew the mind of my children, as they continue to stand.
Open the eyes of my child spiritually.
Make them better, not bitter, as they draw closer to Thee.

Those thought unworthy of forgiveness, continue to drain the soul.
Heal the heart of my children; lest bitterness takes control.
Emotions can overpower, if the flesh is left unchecked.
Memories can be a trigger, bless my children, by Your Spirit, redirect.

Withhold not good from them to **whom** it is due, **when** it is in the **power**
of thine hand to do it.
(Proverbs 3:27)

*W*hen my children are tempted, to be self centered.
*H*elp them to remember, what Christ surrendered.
*O*pen their eyes of understanding.
*M*anifest Your glory, in Jesus's name, as they give, notwithstanding.

*W*ounds can cause one to be bitter.
*H*eal that my children, can be love transmitters.
*E*ven the deep pain, which may reside.
*N*evertheless, increase compassion, in Jesus's name, as they swallow
their pride.

*P*our Your power upon my children, for the flesh is weak.
*O*r they will resort to self, and mistreat the meek.
*W*eapons and wiles, will overcome.
*E*ducation can cause Your wisdom, to seem dumb.
*R*enew their mind, for Your glory, in Jesus's name, lest they succumb.

Withhold not good from them to whom it is due, when it is in the power
of **thine hand** to do it.
(Proverbs 3:27)

*T*hough our Savior has risen, He is on Your right hand.
*H*elp my children understand, where they are to stand.
*I*n Christ's stead, as His hands and feet.
*N*avigating within Your heart, creating an aroma that is sweet.
*E*ating and drinking Your word, in Jesus's name, holy and complete.

*H*ands are for Your glory, for my children, have been brought with a
price.
*A*s they deny self, take up their cross, and follow Christ.
*N*evertheless, by the power of Your Spirit,
*D*irect their steps, in Jesus's name, as they humbly hear it.

Say not **unto** thy neighbour, Go, and come again, and to morrow I will
give; when thou hast it by thee.
(Proverbs 3:28)

Unaccustomed to putting others first, my children may struggle with
generosity.
Nurture and mature, as they seek to trust You; lest they respond in
atrocity.
The blessings You provide, will saturate, and exceed their personal
needs.
Overflow and growth is for peers, coworkers, friends and family.

Prayers for our Children

Say not unto thy **neighbour**, Go, and come again, and to morrow I will
give; when thou hast it by thee.
(Proverbs 3:28)

Natural, self preservation, will lead them to withhold.
Events from the past can leave them bitter, as they forget about their
soul.
I ask that the love of Christ, be spread abroad within their hearts.
Grace them to remember, Christ's intervention on their part.
Heal the wounds, which hinder there perspective.
Bless them with the mind of Christ, as they abide within Your directive.
Open the eyes of their understanding, for Your wisdom will prevail.
Under subjection, let them put their bodies, as they combat the wiles of
hell.
Renew, sanctify, increase hunger and thirst, in Jesus's name, for within
You, all is well.

Say not unto thy neighbour, Go, and ***come again***, and to morrow I will
give; when thou hast it by thee.
(Proverbs 3:28)

Compassion is love in action.
Obedience must be total; not split within fraction.
Maintain a hunger and thirst, for Your righteousness,
Even as self denial, cross bearing, and obedience to Christ is practised,
in Jesus's name, for You are their rest.

Announcing that prayer, will be given and made,
Giving a false promise, without lending aide,
Abandons Your Spirit, which has been given to us.
Increasingly, decreasing, within Christ, is a must.
Nevertheless, direct my children's focus, as they obey Jesus.

Say not unto thy neighbour, Go, and come again, and to ***morrow*** I ***will***
give; when thou hast it by thee.
(Proverbs 3:28)

Making adjustments today, as aide is needed,
Opens the heart of the recipient, to be unimpeded.
Reciting Your word, with little or no action,
Restricts the move of Your Spirit, and minimizes attraction.
Occupy the soul, of my children each day.
Within Christ, in Jesus's name, let sacrifice, suffice, as my children love
Your way.

Will You give a snake, to one who asks for a fish?
Is a stone the answer, to one who begs a cooked dish?
Let my children remember, the love You've shown;
Lest their hearts are hardened, in Jesus's name, set the tone.

Grace my children, with a giving disposition.
I ask that You help them, make Christ like decisions.
Vain are their words, if they fail to walk within love.
Equip them, in Jesus's name, to live within the truth thereof.

Prayers and Praise in Poetic Phrase: Volume Four

Say not unto thy neighbour, Go, and come again, and to morrow I will give; **when thou hast** it by thee.
(Proverbs 3:28)

*W*hen my children, are able to help,
*H*elp them to be able, to set aside self,
*E*ven if it is not convenient,
*N*evertheless, for You've extended grace, which has not been seen yet.

*T*here will be times, that Your words will taste bitter.
*H*ollowed wounds can cause one, to behave as a quitter.
*O*bedience is key, to receive what Christ has granted.
*U*nderstanding is needed, to remain securely planted.

*H*eavenly Father, Your love overflows.
*A*s increase is multiplied, it is for our highs and lows.
*S*o bless my children, to think of others.
*T*each them to have concern, for their sisters and brothers.

Say not unto thy neighbour, Go, and come again, and to morrow I will give; when thou hast it by ***thee***.
(Proverbs 3:28)

*T*he way to life, is through Christ's directives.
*H*ealing manifests, as we adhere, to our Savior's perspective.
*E*ven as they are tempted, to be weary,
*E*mpower my children, in Jesus's name, though their eyes may be teary.

Devise not ***evil against*** thy neighbour, seeing he dwelleth securely by
thee.
(Proverbs 3:29)

*D*uring these days, the love of many grows cold.
*E*motions lead, as passions control.
*V*isions of hatred, can hinder compassion,
*I*f bitterness is allowed to root deep, like a hidden assassin.
*S*ecure the heart of these children of mine.
*E*ven as they seek You, in Jesus's name, abiding within, Christ, the true vine.

*E*ven as enemies align, grace my children, to keep You in mind.
*V*ictory is not measured, by a worldly cosign.
*I*ncrease their spiritual maturity, as they decide to forgive.
*L*et your love motivate, in Jesus's name, how they think and live.

*A*s my children move about their path, offenses will come,
*G*rasping at insecurities, which can reduce a heart to crumbs.
*A*s unforgiveness and bitterness attempts to take root,
*I*ncrease their ability to deny self, that Your Spirit may produce fruit.
*N*eeding the same mercy, that You have gracefully shown,
*S*hape my children's heart of flesh, as they shed their heart of stone.
*T*each them to love mercy, in Jesus's name, as they have known.

Devise not evil against thy ***neighbour***, seeing he dwelleth securely by
thee.
(Proverbs 3:29)

*N*o greater love, exists than this: that a man lay down his life.
*E*ven though we were not worthy, Christ became a living sacrifice.
*I*n times of offence, or during conversations which are intense,
*G*entleness can decrease, as we build a wall of defense.
*H*elp my children recognize, that love is required.
*B*less them to love You, more than anything else they desire.
*O*bstructions, like wounds from the past, can contaminate the heart,
*U*ndermining Your commands, ungodly counterpart.
*R*enew the mind of my children, in Jesus's name, sanctify and set apart.

Devise not evil against thy neighbour, ***seeing*** he ***dwelleth*** securely by thee.
(Proverbs 3:29)

Seeking vengeance, is the flesh, for You will repay.
Emotions move up and down, like the wings of a jay.
Even when provoked, Your standards do not change.
I ask that You strengthen, even when obedience feels strange.
Nevertheless, as their last breath, lead them to hold on, to Your hand.
Grace their thirst, as they remain submersed, in Jesus's name, within Christ's commands.

Daring to take advantage, of ones enemy,
Will cause a disconnection, from You to some degree.
Everyone is to be loved, for You are love.
Lead the heart, of my children, that they may exhibit, fruit from above.
Lead by Your Spirit, for the flesh is weak.
Even as enemies persecute, and operate against the meek.
Teach my children to walk within love, Joy, and peace.
Help them to aide, in Jesus's name, without any malice, in the least.

Devise not evil against thy neighbour, seeing he dwelleth ***securely*** by
thee.
(Proverbs 3:29)

Seasons will change, but You do not,
Even though we have moved, against what Your Spirit has taught.
Controversial conversations, and frustrations, can lead one to vacillate.
Using emotional fatigue, as an excuse, to justify abuse, is Satan's bait.
Regarding Your word, is key to victory.
Even as we remember, that You have shown, unmerited mercy.
Let my children be reminded, that all can be accomplished through Christ.
You are lord of all, hold them; lest they fall, in Jesus's name, suffice.

Teach my children to serve, within the mind of Christ.
Help them to do, it all unto You; lest their faith, seems well overpriced.
Emotions can be moved, by fear and doubt.
Equip my children, in Jesus name; lest they seek success, by earthly clout.

Prayers and Praise in Poetic Phrase: Volume Four

Strive not with a man without cause, if he have done thee no harm.
(Proverbs 3:30)

Seeking to prey upon the weak, simply because one can,
Transgresses Your heart, for Christ died for every man.
Remind my children, of the love You have shown.
Increase their desire, to live the love, that they have known.
Vengeance at times, may be the fruit of Your love.
Even so, bless them to let go, allowing You to repay, the fullness thereof.

Strive not **with** a man **without** cause, if he have done thee no harm.
(Proverbs 3:30)

Withdrawal due to pain, will cripple their direction.
Increase spiritual clarity, for You alone are their protection.
Teach my children to love unconditionally.
Heal their wounds, in Jesus's name; lest their emotions undo Christ-like humility.

Wisdom will cause one, to be at peace.
In spite of a foolish provocation; emotional responses can cease.
Teach my children, to have the mind of Christ.
Heal and reveal Your will, in Jesus's name, as they surrender, to You their life.

Why would bitterness, explode from their mouth?
Is the misunderstanding, worth arguing about?
Tell me, whom shall they convince?
Heal their festering wounds; lest they respond with offense.
Obstructed, but you can wipe away years of tears,
Understanding their doubt, insecurities, and fears.
Touch, in Jesus's name; lest emotions grab the wheel and steer.

Strive not with a man without **cause**, if he **have done** thee no harm.
(Proverbs 3:30)

Cuts are deep, wounds need to heal.
And maturity is a necessity, to push past what they feel.
Use the hurtful events, which have come to pass.
Solidify and edify; lest toxic residue, hinders and harass.
Equip my children, in Jesus's name; lest emotions cause them to
trespass.

Heal the wounds, which have caused them to bleed.
And insecurities, which have been birthed out of need.
Validation is an essential, only You can fill.
Even as my children submit, in Jesus's name, to Your holy will.

Did Able deserve to die? How was Cain offended?
Opposition to their peers, can be their insecurities extended.
Nevertheless, I ask that You'd bless, my children to self reflect.
Even within anxiety, in Jesus's name, grace them to keep themselves in
check.

Prayers for our Children

Strive not with a man without cause, if he have done **thee** no **harm**.
(Proverbs 3:30)

Though David did nothing wrong, King Saul sought to kill him.
Hell was allowed to torture, for Saul was lead, by emotional whim.
Eventually, my children may be, tempted to move within jealousy.
Empower them, for Your glory, in Jesus's name; lest they respond with
hostility.

Herod sought to kill innocent babies.
Alarmed with fear, rumored to be crazy.
Remind my children, that they are secure, within You.
Made an heir, by Christ, in Jesus's name, eternal point of view.

Envy thou not the oppressor, and choose none of his ways.
(Proverbs 3:31)

*E*arthly things are attractive, for they offer satisfaction.
*N*ot only can they hinder my children, but can set off adverse, chain reactions.
*V*ictory belongs to my Children, for within Christ, they overcome.
*Y*ielding to Your word, by Your grace, in Jesus's name, they will not succumb.

*T*here are times, when my children, will be tempted, to envy the oppressor.
*H*eal their wounds; lest they seek worldly means, to relieve their temporal stressors.
*O*pen wide their eyes, that they may grab hold of truth.
*U*nbelief is a thief, bless them to see, in Jesus's name, that Your word renews their youth.

Envy thou not the ***oppressor***, and ***choose*** none of his ways.
(Proverbs 30:31)

*O*bserving the temporal pleasures, that this world does manifest,
*P*erceiving, of the natural, they will seek temporal happiness.
*P*ressing on by faith is, at times, a difficult task.
*R*emind that You empower, with strength and ability, if they would humble themselves, and ask.
*E*ndow them with wisdom, as they surrender every part.
*S*trengthen for endurance, as they seek with their whole heart.
*S*urrender is required, for Christ has called us to self deny,
*O*rdered us to carry our cross, and relinquish self to die.
*R*enew peace and comfort, in Jesus's name, as Your word they apply.

*C*ause my Children to be vigilant, for they have an adversary.
*H*e hates the truth, outside of You, the earthly view, of him is very scary.
*O*vercoming their enemy is possible within Christ.
*O*pposition to believers, draw us closer to eternal life.
*S*trengthen my children as they submit to Christ's commands,
*E*ven as they present their bodies, in Jesus's name, amen.

Envy thou not the oppressor, and choose **none** of his ways.
(Proverbs 30:31)

No one can force pure religion.
Ordered steps are made by decision.
None is perfect, no not one.
Even so, grace my children, in Jesus's name, with the desire, to surrender to Your Son.

Prayers and Praise in Poetic Phrase: Volume Four

Envy thou not the oppressor, and choose none of his **ways**.
(Proverbs 30:31)

When the ungodly seem to prosper, temptation may be near.
And my children will need Your words, to relieve their hearts of fear.
You are able, to exceed expectations.
Satisfy my children, in Jesus's name, as they seek the mind of Christ, in every situation.

For the **froward** is abomination to the Lord: but his secret is with the righteous.
(Proverbs 3:32)

For Your glory, You allowed Pharaoh to harden his heart.
Respect You do our will, for You allow us to rule every part.
Only thing is, it results in damnation:
Wandering out of Your will, increases frustration, and decreases peace within situations.
As my children experience their daily routine,
Renew their minds, as they wholeheartedly cling.
Denying self, for Your glory is a choice, grace my children, in Jesus's name, with more hunger, for obedience to Your voice.

For the froward is ***abomination*** to the ***Lord***: but his secret is with the
righteous.
(Proverbs 3:32)

*A*s the average Pharisee and Sadducee refused to yield.
*B*itten by old testament serpents, the rebellious refused to be healed.
*O*bserving the murmuring and complaints, of the children of Israel,
*M*any lives were lost, for they foolishly opened their mouth, being led
by how they would feel.
*I*n Matthew sixteen, twenty five, Jesus said "whosoever will save his life
shall lose it."
*N*o everlasting peace is outside of Christ, for He is peace, if they so
choose it.
*A*s perilous times increase, for the love of many will wax cold,
*T*each my children to have concern, for their bodies and souls.
*I*ncrease their desire, to have Christ formed within them.
*O*bedience ensures that their, and Your desires become synonym.
*N*urture, for Your glory, in Jesus's name, as they choose Christ's wisdom,
over whim.

*L*ed by emotions, and what they feel,
*O*ppositional, erroneous doctrine, will cripple, wound, and pervert, what
is real.
*R*ebellion is as the sin, of pure witchcraft.
*D*irect and protect, in Jesus's name, as my children remain on track.

For the froward is abomination to the Lord: but his ***secret*** is with the
righteous.
(Proverbs 3:32)

*S*elected, for Your glory, to bare Your holy name,
*E*ven in adversity, they can overcome, because Christ overcame.
*C*itizenship, within Your kingdom, isn't open to all.
*R*equirement: be willing and obedient to Christ's Spirit, who calls.
*E*ven the power to meet this prerequisite, is an ability You've given.
*T*each my children, in Jesus's name, Your secrets of daily living.

For the froward is abomination to the Lord: but his secret is **with** the
righteous.
(Proverbs 3:32)

*W*ith parables Jesus spoke, that the blind would remain blind.
*I*t was Your will, for that day and time.
*T*oday Christ has called for witnesses.
*H*elp my children model, what godly fitness is.

Prayers for our Children

For the froward is abomination to the Lord: but his secret is with the
righteous.
(Proverbs 3:32)

*R*ighteousness is found within Christ alone, for our works are not
enough.
*I*n Him we live, move, have our being, and have access to Your love.
*G*race my children to rest, within what He has done.
*H*eal; lest the wounds of their past, cause them to be overcome.
*T*each them of the requirements, for Jesus has a yoke.
*E*ven of His burden, of which His life evoked.
*O*rder their daily steps, as they seek His mind.
*U*sed their various trials, to enhance a godly paradigm.
*S*anctify them wholly, in Jesus's name, align.

The **curse** of the **lord** is in the **house** of the wicked: but he blesseth the
habitation of the just.
(Proverbs 3:33)

Care is received by all, for Your sun shines everyday.
Under the clouds, we are nourished by rain, for You are good, in every
way.
Reservations, of Your favour, are made for those who follow Your Son.
Satisfaction, for You are able, Is available through only one.
Empower my children, with this knowledge, in Jesus's name, let Your
will be done.

Let grace and truth, in Christ, lead and guide their goals;
Or legalism can condemn, as wiles war against, their souls.
Renew their minds, as they seek with their whole heart.
Direct, in Jesus's name, and protect, as they surrender every part.

Help my children remember, that their body is Your temple.
Obstacles to their rest, keep this practise from being simple.
Unify them with You, as they seek Your face.
Sanctify and satisfy, as they run this race.
Even as they seek to decrease, and give You space.

The curse of the lord is in the house of the **wicked**: but he blesseth the
habitation of the just.
(Proverbs 3:33)

Weapons and wiles, will come to pass.
In and out of season, they desire to hinder and harass.
Continue to protect their hearts and minds.
Keep them pure, within a godly paradigm.
Even as they seek to honor You,
Disciple, in Jesus's name, for Your glory, that they may bare good fruit.

The curse of the lord is in the house of the wicked: but he **blesseth** the
habitation of the just.
(Proverbs 3:33)

Because of Christ, my children are blessed.
Lead, for Your glory, as they seek to enter His rest.
Even as they struggle with consistency.
Secure them by faith unto victory.
Seasons of temptation will come and go.
Empower my children, as they deny their soul.
Teach, by Your Spirit, for instruction is needed.
Heal, in Jesus's name; lest wounds leave them depleted.

Prayers and Praise in Poetic Phrase: Volume Four

The curse of the lord is in the house of the wicked: but he blesseth the
habitation of the **just**.
(Proverbs 3:33)

Having truth, without use, without repentance,
Allows deception, from all directions, to advance its witness.
Bless my children to apply Your word correctly.
Influence they their peers direct and indirectly.
Though they fall short, at times, in one way or another,
As they seek Your pleasure, Your love, joy, and, peace will cover.
The promises are free, for Christ paid the cost.
I thank You that we've overcome, through His sacrifice and loss.
Overcoming by the resurrection, of our Lord and Savior,
Nevertheless, in Jesus's name, grace my children to practise godly
behavior.

Jesus alone saves. He plus nothing else.
Understanding prevents my children, from depending on self.
Satisfy my children, as they seek You, with their whole heart.
Teach, as they reach, in Jesus's name, as they obey Christ's commands,
within every part.

Surely he *scorneth* the scorners: but he giveth grace unto the lowly.
(Proverbs 3:34)

*S*urely their sins will find them out, if they fail to repent.
*U*nlock the truth of Your holy word, as my children seek You, without relent.
*R*escue my children, from the enemies lies.
*E*mpower them to love, even without compromise.
*L*ead them to a closer walk with You.
*Y*ou are able, in Jesus's name, to complete and follow through.

*S*atisfied that there is no judgement, scorners continue, in their way.
*C*aring not for their offence, their wrath grows greater by the day.
*O*ften my children are tempted, for their pit seems to sink deeper.
*R*ebellion will result, unless You are their hope and keeper.
*N*evertheless, You have called my Children to deny,
*E*motional responses, which do not edify.
*T*each my children to give thanks, in all things,
*H*oly living, in Jesus's name, to please the King of kings.

Surely he scorneth the *scorners*: but he giveth grace unto the lowly.
(Proverbs 3:34)

*S*eeking their own way, their pride guides them through.
*C*onsidering not Your word, they do what they choose to do.
*O*f those who have their part, within the lake of fire,
*R*ebellion is their leader, as they seek their own desires.
*N*evertheless, convict; lest my children follow whim.
*E*mpower, for Your glory, that Your word and their desires, become synonym.
*R*eward will be given, according to Christ's commands.
*S*anctify my children, as they purge themselves, in Jesus's name, amen.

Prayers for our Children

Surely he scorneth the scorners: but he **giveth** grace unto the lowly.
(Proverbs 3:34)

Grace my children to receive, Your every word.
Increase as they decrease, though peers think them absurd.
Vanities are present, from without and in.
Empower them to obey, that they may be called your friend.
Teach them to be humble, before You.
Heal, in Jesus's name; lest bitterness from wounds, continuously bleed through.

Surely he scorneth the scorners: but he giveth **grace unto** the **lowly**.
(Proverbs 3:34)

Grant my children with ability.
Revive their souls, as they trust in Thee.
Allow them grace to see their need,
Casting their cares upon You; lest they fall prey to greed.
Empower them, in Jesus's name, that they may serve, Your people, within strength, without shame.

Unto honor, let my children ascend.
Nevertheless, as they repent of every sin.
Teach them to be holy, within and without.
Operating by faith; lest they are moved by doubt.

Let my children see their nakedness, for without You they are bare.
Only You can clothed with righteousness, as they rest within Your care.
When they are tempted to rely on self,
Let love remind them, of their need of Your help.
You are all we need, there is no one else.

The **wise shall inherit** glory: but shame shall be the promotion of fools.
(Proverbs 3:35)

Wise is the one who trusts, within the Son.
I pray that my children, will not exit with their work undone.
Strengthen my children; lest they grow weary.
Educate, within love, in Jesus's name, as they follow after Thee, dearly.

Sharing within our Saviour, is to share His glory.
Hell's gates will not prevail, or strip of heavenly inventory.
Acute self denial and the way of the cross,
Leads to the father, for within Jesus, forfeit is not loss.
Let my children be wise, in Jesus's name, in counting the cost, within
Christ, without shame.

In line for a blessing, as a new creature, within Christ,
Nevertheless, for salvation was bought, with great, matchless price.
Heavenly Father, grace my children to see
Emotions can cloud their identity.
Remembering mistakes of the past,
Increases confusion, for the flesh can distract, hinder, and clash.
Teach my children, in Jesus's name; lest an identity crisis, cripples and
maim.

The wise shall inherit **glory**: but **shame shall** be the promotion of fools.
(Proverbs 3:35)

Grace my children to make eternal investments.
Let love lead the way through godly assessment.
Oder their steps, as they humbly submit.
Remind of Your word; lest they play the hypocrite.
Yes, replenish, in Jesus's name; lest their religion be counterfeit.

Soon all will stand before Christ, to give account,
Having been given talents at various amounts.
And to whom much is given, much will be required.
Make my children aware; lest their faithfulness expires.
Empower by Your Spirit, in Jesus's name, inspire.

Sentence will be passed, for Christ shall return.
Help my children awake; lest they remain unconcerned.
As five virgins were wise, let this be their case;
Lest they fail to prepare, and miss out on their place;
Lest Christ returns as a thief, and they are ashamed to see His face.

The wise shall inherit glory: but shame shall be the **promotion** of **fools**.
(Proverbs 3:35)

Promotion is coming, for Christ shall judge,
Righteously, in holiness, without fear of grudge.
Observing the scriptures; lest their will avoid strife,
Making sure that their words and actions, mirror that of Christ.
Options present themselves, via Spirit and flesh.
These tests and trials, can strengthen and refresh.
I pray that my children, will make wise choices.
Obediently submitted, to that in which the Spirit voices,
Nevertheless, in compliance, to that in which Christ also rejoices.

Functioning as if, they'll give no account?
Obeying the flesh, as if it were paramount?
Observing Your word, with no respect?
Let the ways of this world, be what they reject.
Save my children from themselves; lest Christ's sacrifice, is of no effect.

Prayers for our Children

ABOUT THE AUTHOR

R. J. Shy is the author of Prayers for our children, the forth addition to the series Prayers and Praise in Poetic Phrase series that he began attempting to be a part of the solution. Now, as a full time licensed, ordained Minister of the gospel, he seeks to grow in the grace and knowledge of our Lord, Jesus Christ. He is also seeking to learn how to love his wife, as Christ loved the church, and give his life for her. Mr. Shy and his wife live in the southern, central part of Arkansas.

Answered Prayer Journal

Answered Prayer Journal

Answered Prayer Journal

Answered Prayer Journal

Answered Prayer Journal

Answered Prayer Journal

Answered Prayer Journal

www.ingramcontent.com/pod-product-compliance
Lightning Source LLC
Chambersburg PA
CBHW020511030426
42337CB00011B/331